Molotov:

Poems

Tom Baker

Zem Books

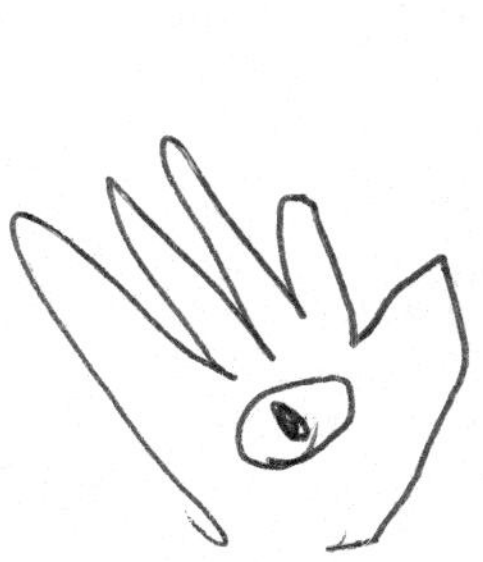

Molotov: Poems

By

Tom Baker

ISBN: 978-1-79480-712-9

Published by Zem Books.

Email: zemrocksme99@gmail.com

Online Store: www.lulu.com/zem66

Like us on Facebook: www.facebook.com/zembooks

Acknowledgements:

Special thanks to those who care and pique my interest, for whatever reason. I would call you out by name--but given the nature of some of the writing herein, I'm afraid you might not like that.

This book is dedicated to my mother, to the memory of old friends gone before, now lost; to all our yesterdays.

Also, to the female EMT who told me she was, "getting ready for me."

You and G-d, honey. You and G-d.

Note:

These poems were all completed years ago. Some of them turned out to be eerily prophetic. This poem, which I dreamed just a few hours ago, is as new as today. Yet, still ancient. And prophetic:

You point your guitar like a gun, and it's black,

Like the clothes on your back, Cowboy--

And you say,

"You want to record a four song EP?"

I have no response but then you laugh again and get up and

Skinny as a rail

Tell me that those bitches will wiggle it for five dollars...

And I'm surprised you're alive again.

While we listen to the Adolescents sing Kids of the Black Hole

And, outside,

There is no more tomorrow but only

Now.

Contents

The Rooster 1

Watch This Mother Burn 2

Jesus Weeping from the Well 4

Joe's Porcelain 6

The Psychopath 8

--this is only a test-- 9

Molotov 10

Curtains 11

Vile 12

The Classroom 13

The Hand 14

Digging for Gold 15

The Letter 17

Gypsies 19

Digging For 21

The Net 23

Violent Men 26

The Animal Grip 29

Fear Writ Large 31

Boat 33

Gator 34

Girl (Dour X) 35

Moon Patrol 36

Thunderbird 37

The Insect Boy 38

The Time-Defying Serpent 40

The Ballad of Bonnie and Clyde 41

Lived in Hell (To Die a Little) 44

The Demon in the Bedroom 46

Drown Silently the Rat 47

Waikiki 49

They Drink MIlk at a Temple of the Rat 51

Light Speed Click 53

Visions O' Great River (Hell on One Bank, Heaven on the Other) 55

Some Fell Among Thorns 57

Auntie's Beach 59

Mama Blowin' in the Breeze 65

Part 2: Recent Poems

Where Have You Been, John Redhawk? 67

Church Bells 70

The Pilot 73

"Rock Around" 74

In the Doorway 77

79 Words and Perfect Fear 78

The Cloth-Covered Form 80

The Window 80

Beef 83

Last Call of the Wild Bird 85

Kill Heyzeus 86

The Body of Ginsberg 87

Black Bird 89

The Ballad of Meat Woman 90

Babel 92

At Carnival 93

Georgia 94

To Johnny Who Thought He Would Never Die 95

Needles 97

The Mankey 97

Raven Number Two 99

The Rooster

I hold your face
in the crook formed by the intersecting
planes of my two palms--
It must be a cinematic angle, a shot for a
feature film
wherein the candid camera is hidden.
Yet, everything, every shot and angle,
seems choreographed to the point of obsessive
perfection.
And Auntie tell me, she say the
"Universe is the vast cosmic egg, wherein
God hath wrought the ins and outs of creation.
And we are a part and parcel of that Cosmic Egg."
But verily I say unto her,
"We don't live on the inside of that egg,
and God lives on the outside surface of the shell.
Perhaps it is the next..."
Wherein...
Planetary systems are hatched by a great--
"Rooster of the Heavenly Spheres!"
But this is all another simple folktale, (...and
so I must cast it aside as intellectual refuse.)
We pop the shell, beyond, then look back
through the crack in the opening exposing a vast
whirling universe
spinning concentrially toward some fulcrum

spot,

        some white hot point building to a really

truly

        evil

        climax...

        When I was a kid you gave me slick, cum-splattered fuck mags to jerk-off to. This was my introduction to sex and the Eternal Mystery. I was the fertilizing agent of your perverse pleasure.

        Now, thirty years and a belly full of revenge later, I want to impregnate the slit in your soul.

        To fill your putrid vulva with the white hot lava of my hate

        And teach you about death, and God, and the Cosmic Egg,

        And other things I know you'll never understand.

Watch This Mother Burn

"There is in every madman
a misunderstood genius
whose idea
shining in his head
frightened people
and for whom delirium was the only
solution to the strangulation

that life had prepared for him. "
—Antonin Artaud

I'll watch this mother burn
    I'll wrap it up around a tattered old
flagpole--
    Hoist it up the line till it does a little
shimmie
Like a convict at the end of a rope dancing in the
flyblown breeze--
    And my, isn't the world hot? What? What?
    If I dip you in shit and set you out on the
tarmac to collect flies
    In your eyes
    Do you even realize that you're just being
used
Another wage slave earning a few crusts while the
fatter and fiestier pigs dance the jig? and they call
it luxuriating in the New Economy that doesn't
include you because, quite frankly, you're just the
shit magnet
    And there're flies to collect
    So if they kill some babies
    or bomb a village
    or turn back the clock to 1863
    or make pretend they are
    holy holy holy eloi lama sabacthani do I
care a whit or damn?

3

No. I'll watch this mother burn,
pornography and all.
I'll watch this mother burn,
its bibles and shopping centers and cheap
diversions --and cooking shows and reality tv
and cyberaugmented fictions of a bourgeois
past that never really existed
beyond reruns of the old and sterile and
false.
My blood bleeds petrol my fingers pop
sparks, And this is all just poetic rumination, so you
can turn down your red flags and knock off the
sirens.
I'm as gentle as a kitchen.
Or a kitten.
Or a cat. With nine lives. Yet still, I tell you,
one sunny day---
I'LL WATCH THIS MOTHER BURN.

Jesus Weeping from the Well

So this house is my inner heart, my
dilapidated chest cavity and herein sit
mister moustache
and ranging about the buggy tattered old
furniture is joe who has been gone for years and
the television is a type of box that spits sparks
and we note we are watching something

4

called Creepshow Three--

But maybe that has something more to do with the three of us sitting here than what is on the

screen

Which is William Shatner playing a bit role dead and someone come on to lick his face, and this is all perverse imaginings and titilating disgust And the horror host pull back a shroud to reveal his legs disappear in the folds of a giant white blob of worm skin

And I pull the television box forward and it slip on the hardwood floor and go poltergeisting around into the darkened causeway which is the living room parlor

I announce is where we continue to watch television

And some little teenage thing in a 1911 gown comes in and she is little, but a fiesty one, and I ask her pointedly if the house is haunted--

No, she say, it's sixty-five years old.

She walk back to the room where the glass windows stare out blackly like eyes. Mr Moustache has nothing in the realm of the intelligible to say. I can't discern it, at any rate-But then I realize that we are straddling two different time frames, and that somewhere on the property, in an old well, a baby skeleton was discovered. And maybe it begins to speak its infant truths through my tongue. And, maybe, just maybe, it was me still in the modern age.

Joe's Porcelain

The house was huge--
    and a cavernous old thing of hollow drips
and black time.
    The tick-tick of dusty years
    echoed miserably across
    the uneven floorboards.
    Outside, the weather cock spins a Vitus
dance in the churning maelstrom of fury, the trees
roaring leaf against stem as the moon illuminates
    patches of dark against bone white truth.
    Inside, I've got a log in each hand and I'm
cowering against the shadow, while Joseph comes
in, his mouth working like a fish, and he's begging
me not to crack the porcelain doll that lay with
infuriating passivity beneath me in the bug-
infested gloom.
    Please he says. I've worked so much he
says. It's not that bad he says. She'll never know he
says.
    But outside
    a peal of thunder and a flash of lightning
lend a specter of the macabre to our surroundngs,

as this dream-like moment in time

--flash-freezes--

in the subconscious flicker of my yesterdays and tomorrows

Too late. All gone. The compassion is spent.

I bring the logs in my arms down, careening with a whoosh through the dead air toward the dying eyes

the button eyes

The black and miserable empty shoeshine sockets

that already know truth because they already know pain...

DO YOU HEAR THAT?

They already KNOW TRUTH, because they already KNOW PAIN.

He's fucked her a thousand times, of course.

Stolen the soul right out and away, to keep, wadded up like a cache of fruit flies captured in the center of his palm, to giggle over.

Please he says. It's okay he says. She likes it he says. It's her time he says.

So I crush the glass cranium, and proceed to devestate the room. Somewhere, in a corner, blinded by the white hot blood red bullet of rage seeping down from one corner of my eye, he cowers in a hole. He's preparing himself for me.

For me. And I'll have him I say.
But not. Just. Yet.

The Psychopath

I'll trap you in the silent cathedral, a place of dour
amusements,
        with pick and rope and bone saw handy to
take your little ego to pieces part by puzzled part,
        with drill bit hammered through splintering
door into the dancing figure
        of the unwilling hostess
        who jibbers in the darkness
        at the injustice of it all.
        This love is a madness born within, the
sickness they say I can never shake, and with hands
in grubby pockets I peer beneath beard to see the
game being played by Sacred Mother in the dust.
        And this place they've set apart for us,
beyond reach of newspaper jackal and tired blue-
suit eye
        is perfect in the way that a thigh bone
crushed
By the speculation of a weight imposed is perfect
in the way it pops.
        I cower in the darkness,
        crouched above booby trap,
        swinging the noose,

waiting for that first rustle of feet through door to know your tired gaze and slack mouth of regret.

You can write all the missives you want to the pecking vultures of public opinion, parade with placard in the streets and denounce the demons that damn you until judgment or sunrise
whichever comes first,
but this darkness is mine and eternal, and in here I am breathing
and waiting
and the only power in the world is this fist
and what it can claim.

--this is only a test--

Cackling like witches at a Sabbath,
Dancing in the blue fire of ferocious Luminosity,
Working strange magic with heavenly vulva pressed against the dim, choked mouth of Father Sky-
I know that I can touch you, in deep grooves of old oil
As the dry cracked surface parts for the feeling grip
of my brain to scan the picture of an old fighter grown victorious
in the ringside seat of dreams-

And this is only a test.

(What jungle drums pound heathen muzak
for the immortal soul

Of this esbat?

None, and I reckon that pictures are all I
have...)

Molotov

Out beyond the railroad tracks-

in the dip that rises and falls along the edge
of the road-

as we move through bumpy

streets talking JFK,

I note that young anarchists

with Molotov minds

are planning a symbolic gesture of defiance-

And I make sure and explain

that Operation Mongoose

happened in New Orleans

with anti-Castro Cubans,

and we laugh as we drive

because ahead of us a passel of girls has
dropped a bottle

and is running like mad to escape the
flames,

but a jacket has caught the spark of the
wind and in a few steps

one bursts into fire
still running-
and it is the most amazing thing I have ever
seen!
and I laugh again
because empty gestures
fill me with contempt,
and I note that that girl
is going to look grotesque
once somebody puts her out.
But maybe she was just filled
with the fire of righteous indignation, and I
think that youth,
running madly in the breeze,
could be filled with fire
and nurtured on heat
and that bursting into flame
might be the most sensible thing in a world
gone mad-
and I wake up and write a few lines About
this senseless dream.

Curtains

It's a bolt from the theatre for me, as I am
alone in the audience, not wanting to glimpse
your sagging elephant flesh
as the curtain parts.

My footfalls land like heavy pebbles on the surface of the moon,
and this carpet is like flypaper as I move out the glass doorway, past the screaming woman,
and into the fog.
Through the wrought-iron gate
and glancing up at a window
two dark shadows move beyond touch of floor lamp as the men start in their places, and I know that this is for real.
I really am a monster, and she really is my victim.
Jack the Ripper is born.

Vile

Sucking the vile stick
You sit on the pot
While Nine Inch Nails

Hammers away in the background.
I am naked
As is he
Who, alone, can make the disgust I feel for you
Seem so palpably real.

The Classroom

Pouring libations for the classroom
I stop to consider that the project-
    which is little more than a paint-by-
numbers rose
torn from a sheaf of coloring books-
    may not suit the mental aptitude of the
assembled students.
    Wine flows freely from plastic jugs, and I
look so smashing in my new suit that I hardly mind
being instructed to complete someone else's
project, an obscure coloring dotted with
    arcane scribbling,
    and someone complains to me that
education, whatever
    else it is, may not be suitable for a tough
kid with a
    mohawk and "No Future!" poised
somewhere to burst forth
    back of his throat,
    and I notice that the girl, that eternal girl
who transforms
    herself nightly to suit my longing, is sitting
in the back row,
    and I go to her, and tell her 'I love you, and I
always will love you,"
    but she merely smiles

and her teeth look like jagged chips of rock.
"I know," she says. "But-"

The Hand

A gnarled hand of stone reaches up out of the field, grasping the clear blue sky above the roof of the old place.

Someone has parked a building, from a city long ago, across the way from the neighbors;

twin ghosts peer out of dusty windows.

1902 suits and ties that look like nooses as black men wave from tenement rooftops to white boys

in the fields below. "Holler back if you can hear us!"

This dirty building, dusty, dank-covered in soot and years- does not belong here,

but time has doubled over into a knot.

Who are these daguerreotype faces, who these dusky smiles, that make decades vanish

with flutter of waving fingers?

The boys do not know the answer to this but outside in back of the house an airplane star bolt shoots

in heavenly splendor.

"Can't you hear it buzz?" asks one but the

light betrays the origin from many galaxies away,
        as neighbor kids chase airborne red disc
down.
        (hopscotch sidewalk)
        A solid rectangle of infrared shoots down
the neighborhood,
        feeling faces that are being scanned to
learn the measure of time.
        And no wonder the past vomits up a
present for the future...

Digging for Gold

Digging for gold in the blackest night
While all around me, framed in the windows
overlooking the courtyard,
        Murder leaps out the jaws of a hungry lion,
To devour dead man sitting, with a knife in the
forehead,
        Hammered against the kitchen tiles.
        A boy bites down on a rare gold doubloon,
Smiling to know the taste of wealth,
And factories lean crazily at angles over dripping
alleyways
        As I examine a stain on the map.
        "It's here! It's here!" yells an old man,
Leaning crazily on a shovel

Over what he believes is a buried treasure
ripe for the plucking.

But I don't know,

Perhaps we have simply mixed our
coordinates,
With strange frequencies beamed in over the
mental wireless

That brought us to this mound of earth to
start with.

Dying babies howl in the steam whistle of a
locomotive,

Suffering lost in the pathetic cries and
grinding crunch of train track chomp

As the night plays out its final shuddering
gasps.

Doorways lead to nowhere,

But not quite to evidence

Of a brutality that was exhibited
On the body of a victim

By a fat woman with a crust of sandwich
Chomped in her jaws.

And I am alone under street lamps / That
are coming down around me in pools of white

As bugs circle crazily zigzagging under the
bright canopy

Of electric wave.

And a wind from somewhere plays down
the street

And I feel a cold chill of purpose
And I realize that, despite the treasure under my heels,
    I am poor and alone.
    Somewhere, an organ grinds...

The Letter

Sunrise is a foul bitch
Wiping the dreams from my mind
Like dusting cobwebs at dawn.
    I expected more from a night's wanderings
Than you in the hospital
    And me sending a gourd in an envelope.
    Did the fragile seeds remind you that there
really is a God?
    Did I tell you as a boy about the rules
concerning smoking?
    How things change in the dim vista of years
 As the struggle continues
    Unabated?
    Perhaps your condition isn't terminal, And
perhaps your need for truth outweighs my clinging
to falsehood.
    No matter, you returned my message with
scotch tape and derision
    Stamped on the outside of an envelope

that could contain the world.

What was I trying to say?

That hope is a mirthless, tired whore shaking herself awake at dawn?

That we all need a dream to cling to as the bitter acid of minutes erases boyhood charm from our sagging features?

I'm feeling old today, and the creaking furniture of bygone sunsets isn't being sold in my personal store of memories and delusions.

In fact, I'm feeling used today, like fate that motherfucker has turned me out onto a street lined with sad faces and tired eyes.

(How much will you pay for me to comfort you?

I could write missives from now until Judgment.

Would you listen, ensconced as it were, in your comfortable stiff bed and starched white shroud?) Decadence suits you, even in the enfolding arms of your ultimate demise.

And death of this dream is permanent delusion.

I'll take the letter back.

I'll eat my own damn fruit.

I'll shove it down my throat until I choke, and then laugh as I vomit up bits and pieces of guilt.

I'm not your own to tamper with, nor can
use be made of a carcass so willing to spoil itself on
the
bright white sands of burning enmity.
This confession has meant nothing.
Tomorrow night you'll be well, and I'll be
sick.

Gypsies

Last night I fell in with a family of gypsies
Driving a beat-up old station wagon across the
Width and breadth of the American Night.
We watched a film of fat ladies
Frolicking at a circus
Freaks and carnival people surrounding us
On a couch that must have been made of
Solid stuff.
Mother and Father worked a restaurant,
Junior wore his boots and belt proudly,
Baby girl sat in the back munching
French fries
And the family dog was a noble, obedient mutt.
I felt like I had finally come home,
And realized that, inside myself,
I long to wander
Wondering at the spectacle of
Life as it is displayed in rich pageantry

19

By the poor and elect.

       But no man could work a more serene
magic
 Than to dream a dream of family
       As that is all we ever know
 On our trip from birth to death,
 And back again.
       Sunrise beckons a stiff back to yearn for a
yoke,
A maiden to give vent with anguish
As daylight strikes the handsome face of demon
lover,
       Circling above, birds see more than we can
ever know,
       As landscape dissolves in the eternal
American backdrop
       Of faded stores and dusty doorway,
countertop dramas played out
       For poor shekels
       In the caravan dirt.
       Brightly painted the dull cloths of sunset
attractions
       Beckon curious throngs to see the Half
Man, the Fat Lady, the Porpoise Boy,
       For a nickel we can dream you nightmares
and idle fancies-
       A dull way to escape,
       Staring into the prism of another's tainted

flesh.

      But freaks are understood by God as the
last representations

      Of a mischievous handiwork,

      Unsettled, wandering, yearning against the
grey

      clouds of a world,
That spits in cold derision at their passing.

Digging For

      Flipping through the songbook, singing the
same dire tunes,

      over and over again.

      I see your gun drawn under shadow of
grizzled face,

      whiskey breath,

      sitting on the piano

      you might even resemble

      Old Stagger Lee.

      Speak to me in dreams and visions, but
don't raise your voice;

      my nerves can't handle it.

      I feel a little shaken.

      Could you shoot straight as a note of music,
played badly,

      on a recording running in reverse?

      Is the music of our lives a cacophonous

blending of bone crunch notes blasted into the
firmament of sunrise?

I can't dream you Colonel,

as soft as a Kentucky downpour,

warning the black man about a plot to
murder his children.

Somewhere,

in the siren wail of a passing train,
loneliness stills the panic

as I drain the last dregs from my cup.

I am looking for an image.

(I am seeking a pale treasure, haunted by
the realization that slow words ring hollow, as I
type out my waxen effigy of little spaces and droll
dots.) Couldn't I form you out of mental clay, and
erect an idol that could laugh, and sing, and cry
and perplex,

and solidify this straggling poem until the
image bursts,

like dire sunrise,

through the cloud covering of my
benumbed skull?

Where is my image?

Where is my music?

Haunted hallways beckon nature to creep,
like straggling tendrils of time, through the
boarded windows of the soul;

Time is not a friend to me, I do not walk

with it
in shadows cast by the yawning mouth of a
stone monument called
"All Our Days".
Instead here I sit, bleached white as a
midnight bone,
tucked into the comfort of cold walls where
hate dwells and knows me for the coward that I
am.
The dream will not leave me.
I cannot see my image.
I do not hear the music.
But my fingers work restlessly at the keys
because they must.
They must.
I am digging for something grand.
I am hunting treasure in the back brain.
I am picking my mental nose.
I suppose...

The Net

The net.
I'm caught in the net,
Captured like a fish;
Trying to breathe the air
Up here is not healthy; My lungs could

burst at any time.

You and I discuss whys and wherefores,
(Was punk better when it was slower or faster?)
And yet we cannot emerge at a consensus at what
constitutes reality.

Perhaps because this is only a dream, And
you'll only exist for the few seconds it takes me to
blink open and tumble over,
Roll out of bed, and decide that the fish is better
off alone,

Rolling through the distant waves,

"Sea bound and sunlight dappled, emerging
through the crest of a churning splash as leaps of
narcolepsy send the cable of thought down
through inky fathoms to emerge, once more, with
something at the end of an almighty hook."

And that hook is thought. And speared at
the end of it is Dream. And Dream is the world.

(And like a fisherman I toss the net back
out, hoping for a bite, waiting for release, my
thoughts flowing easily like the waters of a
sumptuous sea, and knowing full well that, as fish
is to man, Dream is to Idea.)

As fish is to man, Dream is to Idea.

As fish is to man, Dream is to Idea.

(But really we all weave our own webs, toss
about in our own nets, capture ourselves in the
flashbulb moment of our ideas of truth and

beauty.)

    I could tell you a legend,

    I could bring the barnacled corpse of an
idea to life,

    Could send the revenant out searching for
his love

    To hold in watery arms,

    Desiccated flesh dripping with lichen,
As he steals her beneath the waves
 And we lose sight of this b-movie tableaux
beneath inky blackness of roiling water.

    But this is only the ghost of a tale, And I am
in no mood for haunting.

    Let the dead bury the dead,

    And the fish swim in the sea,

    And the ideas drop in dreams like tears in a
winter rain;

    I've had enough of you,

    Twisting about,

    Captured,

    Sordid boot stomps across a factory floor,
Construction worker taunts the ideas of a burning
vision,

    Wolf whistles at phantasm flicker,
 Bald head erect and walking the deuce step angry
chomp of a television bigot.

    Open the box;

    It looks like a head.

Shaped like a thought.
Buried like an idea.
Step inside,
One little foot,
And feel the net close about you.
Captured like an animal,
Lifted for a dry crucifixion,
Struggle,
Scream,
"I'm caught! I'm caught! I'm caught!"
It is just a dream...

Violent Men

Seventy violent men,
With all their talk of action,
Their coats of arms,
Their medals and medallions
(Ribbons chafed with blood, Boots coated
in pork)
Couldn't relieve me of the burden
Of writing this book
Which isn't even mine own
Handiwork.
I found you on a shelf,
(I don't need to ask the pregnant poetic
question)

In a library filled with tears,
But that's not quite right:
It was a bookstall of idle nighttime fancy,
A place conjured on the wisps of a dreaming mind,
Nurtured on the possibility of publication,
Of ersatz material anthologizing
The exploits of the elect.
Do our dream books exist
In some alternate sphere;
Some reality that we cannot conceive
Just over the horizon?
Does the apocalyptic tome
(And now I have slipped back into
interrogation)
Portend a real and true Final Hour that sits,
Curled like the sleeping dragon of the ages,
Waiting to belch flame and mortars and rounds
Of slinging gunfire at the hordes of the
rabble,
"Who perch at the edge of nightmare
bookshelves
To see if they can glean the answer to a riddle
they've never been asked?"
All of this is perplexity.
The night before I was in prison.
My occupation was chiefly the repair of
fractured clocks,
Strange little diodes that told some

inscrutable time,

Before the vast, churning steamroller of empty corridors "...and hallways that penetrated into the bowels of a cavernous, subconscious recess."

I am the Institutionalized Man.

I am not an Action Arm,

I hold not a bloody scythe,

I've read Redbeard but that's as far as I've evolved,

From marshmallow softness,

To bold calculation.

So I made a jailbreak

(still looking for that weeping library?)
To run alongside the grinding wheels of Spectral locomotive

And not to be trapped and severed

Like Elizabeth Short
By those vast rubber tires.

(Even a bindle stiff has nerve endings.) But I've forgotten the whys and wherefores...

Did I make it out alive?

I couldn't say.

But seventy Action Men,

With bold arms,

Holding bloody swords,

Couldn't fill the pages of a book, I know that I will never write.

The Animal Grip

(It spreads across the land like the
rusticated bones of some prehistoric monster.
    Empty hallways still echo
    the nighttime uttering of passing ghosts.
    Megaliths of steel and concrete rise into
the blue heavens,
    cast under the sun like the runic symbols of
some bygone age, to stand like sentinels against
the bulwark of voracious TIME.)
 Step lightly through the empty streets.
    Make little noise as echoes rebound with
haunting integrity.
    Can you hear the whispers of yesterday
Circle your ears,
    As you contemplate the painted stripes
On a bed of asphalt?
    This is the final monument to our grandeur.
    This is our pagan folly.
    This is the dinosaur of our endeavors.
    Empty, void, alleyways that criss-cross
Like psychic vortices,
    To the center of an abandoned shopping
mall
In Des Moines.

Across the campus,
A building with broken windows leers like
rusted teeth
Through the smile of jagged glass.
A marble fountain belches up a statue of a
little angel
Who will never again spray moisture
Across the mossy stones of so many pitched coins.
This may be the final citizen,
Frozen forever in a moment of blissful realization,
That the world is alone.
(Signs betray restaurants and ice cream
parlors, book stalls, and clothing stores. But the
customers have faded into the dying
reverberations of yesteryear, and the good times
no longer roll.)
Will an alien race,
Find this,
In a thousand years,
Like some archeologist discovering the ruins
of Troy,
And wonder:
Why is it these people drove red cars,
Ate iced cream,
And lived for a single, absurd moment, In
the sunshine prism,
Of a yesterday that never was?
But concrete grooves and lonely walls are

wailing in the distance,

As buildings slumber under the animal grip of night.

(Where is everybody?)

Fear Writ Large

All I know is wretched fear,
My old friend shooting from the chest,
Like a piffling ache that wants to be born
Into pain.

Sleep disturbed by nothing,

Dreams sacrosanct prisms of fantasy,
Yet I cannot control the brainwash images,
The sad illusions,

Of my slumbering hours.

And I know the taste of FEAR.

Writ large in icy letters that drip anticipated blood.

Did you leave me in the forest of that longing domicile,

(Surrounded on all sides by the cemetery walk,
The séance parlor,

The dead cards held aloft in trembling hands)
As the pale and silent throng wing out into an

infinity
      That will disappear with the sunrise wide
open gaze of my
      Rheumy eyes?
      Sing a canticle for me,
      Delight in my poison,
      I am bereft and still and alone in the room,
      Where the spirits speak to old friends in
muted tongues,
      And I breathe in the stale air,
To know that Father waits for you, as like as not a
dead hand,
      Holding down the tarot of our lives,
 As each body blinks out into the mists of merciless
time.
      And what I know is FEAR,
      And how I feel the regret wash over me,
And take me,
      And poison me,
      And distort my sleeping fancies until light
and life seem
      Filtered through the branches
      Of a brooding tree.
      (And it is there my body hangs.)
 Goals
      I have goals,
      What next?
      Will I ever know

What it is like to live like the rich man?
Or am I forever condemned to be a shiftless
mouse,
Pecking at the rancid cheese
Of a pretended life?
Will I ever swoon like Romeo
Before the awesome visage
Of some svelte Juliette,
As I try and reconcile
My past failures with my future ones?
Will I groan to know the weight of
Silver treasures and golden fragments glistening,
Like pyrite embers in front of my Gluttonous eyes?
Does this longing charm you?
Are you a snake?
Do you twist in a basket?
Am I a flute?
(I demand sanity trials and a hung jury…)

Boat

This boat is a part of me,
An extension of who I am;
And maybe you can't see that the boards
are my bones,
The waves are my blood,
The rudder is my brain,

And the destination is a few nautical miles,
From the center of my soul.

Gator

    I can't contain this savagery

    So lie atop me

    Biting your underbelly to suffocate me

With your mountain of tall flesh; I'll rip your throat
you white motherfucker,

Send your bulk across the bed of the car And you
laugh and say,

    "You cannot win against me!"

    But I will

    With twisted hook of knife

    I'll meet you and Lady Love in one, many

showers To make a scene from a Hitchcock thriller
Seem pale and bland by comparison.

    Taking the blade,

    cutting the flesh,

    sizing up my options,

    I walk stealthily around the gun shack and

see what a monster you've become.

    Lizard hide,

    reptile man,

    eating the snout and guts

    of the gator,

you've mutated into a hopping nightmare
but I am ready.
The threat of this dream coalesced into a
yawning absurdity,
I state unequivocally that I will spill your
blood.

Girl (Dour X)

Last night I dreamt of a beautiful girl
Resplendent before me-
Nude and vulgar-
Bathed in terrible scents that gave birth to
Thoughts of biology.
This shunned mistress bent and scissored
Like a trapeze contortionist
With her delicacy hefted into the air For all
to see.

***

Paint your dour X
On the wall
In magic marker
Stains of old time
As we move out
Reckless

To the music that they cannot hear
Tired cops
    Chase us through alleyways
    Dripping our names,
And revolution waits
    On the tip
    Of a baldheaded tongue.
    Arise nihilist, take your pleasure
At the strings of a bass
    Tortured to feedback bursts
    As the Dalai Lama expounds
    To us
    Western Buddha perfected!
    (Am I a journalist now?)

Moon Patrol

Heaped piles of garbage, litter of old
fragments left behind to rot, colors cascading in
merciless array across cartoon images of dying
baby T-shirt emblazoned with MOON PATROL
    (--Brain scan reveals that subject is
obsessed with Patty Hearst--)
    Riding the King's Highway across bone meal,
moving mountains of cat flesh, demolition derby of
the dying brain,
    spinning out of control at the gun shop,

fighting the senseless war in China and marrying
the mail order bride in frozen trailer parks to
Peking,
        dreams and nightmares solidified, stand
exultant
        I LIVE!

Thunderbird

        Drums along the river speak to me,
Dancing pow-wow of the mind,
        While somewhere in the night,
        He beckons with wings outstretched--
        The miraculous thunderbird,
        Fabled old dinosaur of yore
        Swooping down with terrible purpose
On some mission of destruction that will claim the
life
        Of exactly one young girl.
        Indian maidens dance burnished around icy
fire
 As Alaskan wind howls in the cold winter night--
        Knowing the rise of legends come in from
the tired mouth
        Of yesterday's wagging tongue.
        The body of knapsack hugging cadaver,
Lying still in the house after winged horror

Swept penultimate among the assembled.

Carrying knife in pocket with switchblade sensibilitiy

The policewoman investigates the death while the tribe titters to know that sometimes old monsters never lose their bite.

The Insect Boy

The boy had an enormous head, and the crowds lined up to "ooh!" and "ah!", and the money was flowing into the coffers of the freak show impresario. What's more, the boy had tremendous black eyes that seemed as deep and dark as obsidian pools. People didn't like to stare into his face; they felt like they could get lost in those eyes.

The boy, for his part, had no other idea how he was to get along in the world. Ever since he had crashed here, a year ago, he had been strongly aware that he looked startlingly different than the natives on this dirtball planet. So all he could do was pose as a freak and put himself on display.

But that was fine.

He had met some fine people: midgets, hairy men, pinheads, fat ladies, clowns, and even a "blockhead" who hammered nails into his nose and ate broken glass. These people were

38

his new family, and he was thankful for them.

He also liked the food here plenty. Cotton candy, hot dogs, corn dogs, soda--it was all good stuff. Of course, it sometimes gave him a belly ache, but he often overindulged in these treats, so he guessed it was his own fault.

* * *

He came out onto the stage, wearing his hood, and Tommy was talking him up for the crowd, getting them worked up, and all of a sudden he took off the hood and he could hear people gasp in the audience. He looked out as a few women and at least one man fainted, and he smiled his thin little smile. This was always the best part of the night.

Later, after the crowd had trickled out and the midway was rolled up and put away for the evening, he would go out into the dust and look up at the stars, and somewhere out there wonder if his people, whom he assumed were looking for him, would one day come to take him home.

And his great black eyes would shed a few tears, and he would say to himself (just like he had heard in a movie), "There's no place like home, there's no place like home, there's no place like home..."

The Time-Defying Serpent

On that final day
Will we stand,
Like supplicants
In a temple of light,
While still they fly
In naked splendor
Lighting up the worlds?
Did your hooked cross
Spill blood into the firmament
For Eve, while dragon
Borne of woman
Measured the distance
Between constellations?
Do they yawn below,
Or beckon from above?
Children of God,
Or of the Python?
Mighty snake eating its own tail,
Ourobouros,
The time-defying serpent hissed Into the
yawning void.

From "You Can't Win" by Jack Black (1926):

"I didn't call them suckers or saps because they were different and worked for a living. They represented society. Society represented law, order, discipline, punishment. Society was a machine geared to grind me to pieces. Society was an enemy. There was a high wall between me and society; a wall reared by myself, maybe-I wasn't sure. Anyway I wasn't going to crawl over the wall and join the enemy just because I had taken a few jolts of hard luck."

The Ballad of Bonnie and Clyde

Bonnie and Clyde sat on the bed, trying on their parents' clothes.

(Clyde was born for trouble, I knew, and Bonnie was sure to follow.)

Little arms, thrust through sleeves too long and too loose.

But eventually, they seem to have found clothing that would fit-

-I like this, I like this, I like this, too...

(Bonnie liked everything.)

Two women working at a table, as I notice Clyde gets up to exit, stage left.

He leaves a bundle of paper notes with his Bonnie. Bills, filthy lucre; ill-gotten gains.

I'm supposed to transfer this collection of documents in the morning. The women are sorting them out in two piles. Right and left, like my politics...

-I want them divided into equal parts. I want them paper-clipped.

-Cost you SIX DOLLARS.

-What? For a paperclip?

Neither of them are smiling, but their busy fingers are folding and arranging as they stand at the long table.

I feel impatient, look around the place.

Where the hell is this sordid basement located?

I note piles of cast-off old clothing in the corner. I also note the general sordid, dingy condition of these underground rooms.

Angrily, I pick up an armful of musty, moth-eaten wares, and thrust them through the curtained (by an itchy old blanket) narrow doorway of the adjoining room.

I do this until the pile disappears. As I work, I make that a few interested parties seem to be milling around in the next room.

(What's going on back there?)

I peer inside, my eyes adjusting to the darkness.

Bonnie and Clyde lie dead in sickening tableaux; Bonnie's skinny legs spread wide, white stockings pulled up to her bloodied waist, traveling up streaked thighs while Clyde, his hat falling off his head in a torrent of brains, lies beside her.

(Was someone still clutching a gun?) Teeth bloody, streamers of red paint white, mannequin visages raw with power and force of death image.

Little pilgrims at the Temple of Self-Damnation.

Two responses:

1. I reel backward in the dark, not knowing, exactly, how everything I've seen fits logically together.

2. Put my hand over my mouth, vomit copious brownish white bile, looks like chicken gravy.

I peer over, not really sick as much as surprised. I look down at the spreading puddle of puke, see something solid and roundish floating down there.

Bend over with trembling, weak fingers to pick it up.

At first, I make it's some sort of toy football helmet. Then I realize with numb horror: It's a baby's skull.

I linger mentally over the image of Clyde's coconut head crushed under the impact of a bullet punctured his cheek...hair standing on end, face swollen in rigors of killing agony. Bonnie's face is elated, ghoulish mask of smile as her stiffened head tilts back.

(Did Mr. Death make love to her in her final moments?)

There's a large B/W photo of Bonnie's funeral repose hidden in a bundle of those papers. But I didn't know that just yet.

Lived in Hell (To Die a Little)

It is a mirthless life,
Lived in hell,
Yet in spite of tears and trials,
I succumb not to the blandishments of Space,
But the infinitude of Time.

***

I am defaced, neutered; a recalcitrant dog.

My heirlooms of self-pity do not fit; I do not want them.

Take these rusted vestiges of my horror
away, I cannot stand the eager tramp of time.
Lost, decayed, forgotten,
Is this what it is worth to live?
Do we recede against the grey mists of
time, Or do we swell like a burgeoning sea?
Is our soul tossed and turned like a sleeper
before the sunrise?
Or do we die a little every day to know the
dawn?
I am stifled in my attempts to clear the
cobwebs of hoary falsehoods
Away from my eyes,
To see the true nature of things as they
reside, In unglamorous entropy,
On the bare mists of mother earth.
And I hear the wail of a siren call called
DEATH
Which beckons to me like a grim mirage.
Will I in that last instant know the bitter
sting of regret?
Or will the healing balm of truth wash me
like a spare orphan,
As I am embraced in the unloving folds of
yet another dream?
Dismal eyes see the darkness with pure
intent, Know the hard and angry truths of life, Do
not regret the sunrise,

And do not worship the sunset.

Though its beauty be a golden spun
embrace of purest fancy,

I would know the hard truth of life
Before I would succumb to that meandering
romance of existence

That prophets tell us wipes our tears away.

The Demon in the Bedroom

Both men are ready to stab each other, In front of
the girls;

It's a form of competition best left to
animals.

There is blood everywhere,

Hack and slash;

"But we are brothers," one protests lamely,

"And there is no sisterhood of women."

They decide that killing each other is
meaningless;

Better to explore the boundary
Between male and female,

Sex and power,

Domination and submission.

But somewhere,

A leering devil,

A burning demon,

A lustful bogey,

Is looking in a mirror and not liking the situation.

("I've tortured striplings in the womb," he thinks, "yet I cannot move these fools to killing each other. There must be a way to rectify this situation. I won't be satisfied until blood is flowing freely between them.")

"What a handsome Devil I am, worthy of a portrait!"

The demon thinks that it is time to intervene.

He moves upward through tunnels of blackness, To seat himself on the edge of a bed, With four people

Who no longer seem to be

Spattered in grue.

Drown Silently the Rat

Drown silently the rat,
Let him creep mysterious,
Through moats of darkness,
Wells of deepness,
Until he burrows,
Like a purposeful mole,

Straight through the recesses of my heart,
To rest somewhere back of the rusted cogs,
Of my dreaming brain.

***

I snuffle up through cottony layers of slumber,
Revolted by the continuum of dream images
 Which I cannot approximate;
I have apparently moved to a house Of
immense dimensions,
Occult proportions: Nightmare staircases
that lead from hexagonal landings,
Down hallways that end in blank walls of
solemn wood,
Beneath cavernous ceiling implanted with
dour brown purpose.
All is dark here, desolate, and perhaps
revenge is foremost on the minds of everyone
involved.
I am apparently here to watch television,
(There is a television tuned to a fuzzy channel) I
can't make out the picture,
It could even be a news report...
I'm sure that it's a movie however.
I'm joined by two girls. Two little minx
foxes. One of them looks like an...
My mother seems to be here. Everything is

confusion, but I try to focus on the movie.

On the fuzzy television set.

And the two girls take turns trying to kick me to death.

And this is not a game. This is sucking from me the life pain as the socked little feet go thump thump into my chest and pelvis again and again...

And I still don't know where the hell I am, Or what I am doing here.

And we are all of us lying on the wood floor, and

I try to swim back up through that cotton sea of sleep, and I think, "Well, that's a woman for you."

Waikiki

I went back in the back room,
To get a look at my bedroom
After being gone for all these years.
-Somebody in there painting, she said.
-Trying to fix that place up.

Indeed, I went down the hall, entered, saw a man in coveralls with a paint roller on a stick.

He was going over the walls carefully. But then I noticed something:

49

The walls were still pitted, covered in little plastic thumbtacks. The thumbtacks must have been used to hold up the posters and other detritus that still clung in nasty array

Like the bygone trophies of some Obsessive snippet collector.

-He would have been better off with a scrapbook, I thought. Then I realized that the clippings were all yellowed newsprint from MY TIME.

My childhood collections.

My posters.

There was a clipping from an old friend of mine, something he had written for the high school newspaper.

I wondered at this, why whoever had occupied this space had just left those old pieces of newsprint tacked up on the wall

...and had I really collected all of this?

I suddenly glanced up at a poster high on the wall. It was a teenage pop princess from a bygone era. Had she been on a popular situation comedy at one point?

She was wearing a brown bomber jacket, had long brown hair, delicate features, a pale complexion...

I don't know why, but, for some reason, I found myself mentally referring to her as Waikiki

Even though that certainly wasn't her name.

They Drink Milk at a Temple of the Rat

We two in bed staring at the ceiling; Only a streak of moonlight illuminating the heavy black ink that swallowed up the ceiling.

The house is dark and dank and hot.

-And unsafe, she reminds me, propping herself up on one arm.

A buxom creature with frizzy, loose curly hair, an ample bosom and a little fat.

An approximation of someone I've known before.

(Toni?)

Next to us, lying as stiff and cold as a board, drawing flies,

Grandma dead as a doornail...

But looking none the worse for all that.

Curiously animate.

I am too scared to move

But I must ask, -Did we?

And the buxom Missus says, -You're not sure?

Did we...what?

Drawing it out with an insinuating sneer
And I hear rats nibbling in the corners of the room
And realize this house really is abandoned,
left to rot in this crime-infested ghetto hell where
All our happy memories of yesterday were beaten
and robbed.

-We shouldn't even be here, I remind her.

Grandma rises from her deathbed like
Nosferatu, Lifting straight up, almost without
bending, coming to life as if she were a puppet to
be plugged in to an electrical socket.

The flashlight in her hand dips a steady,
illuminated pull around the dusty, cobwebbed
murk.

Tiny pitter patters of little racing feet and
colliding tails thump against the rotten
wooden floorboards.

Grandma has on her dusty best
But not what she was buried in; It's an old
number she wore many decades,
With no hose and old, patchy sneakers.

She bends over, shines the flashlight on the
baseboards,

Says, -You can see where they've nibbled
away the wood. Probably the wiring too.

-No wonder we're wandering around here
in the dark. I intone, my arm closing around the
buxom lass shivering next to me in the darkness.

52

Grandma has a mad, marble face, and full lips.

I imagine she drinks blood.

-It's not a good time to turn on the electric, she says. She seems to be incapable of doing anything but grinning in a manner quite macabre (Also, I think, ghosts don't like the light...) I begin to think about Satanic plagues, rats as harbingers of the presence of evil...

But in India, the Buxom One reminds me, *they drink milk at a Temple of the Rat...*

We make love in the same bed, grit of grave dirt stinking up the sheets,

And Grandma lies as stiff as a board beside us,

And like a leech, she may be draining the spiritual sustenance of US, in this house

Condemned as it is

To an eternity

Of rotting wood.

His head lolled to one side as he sped along.

Curiously, he could compare his present state to playing a computer simulation.

Light Speed Click

Standing resplendent as a fleshed jewel

53

At the top of the ramp
      leading down
      From the fuselage of the strange ship
His face a running miasma of butchered parts
Slopped together like some Frankenstein visage of
chopped
      Liver and grue;
      One eye popping
      Like an insectile bullseye
      From the mucky pyramid of this alien head
 He titters to command the Captain Lofty, majestic,
King of the Galaxy
His enemies amassed in cosmic freighters
Waiting to bomb the homeworld far above
 The Captain commands,
-MY ORDERS ARE TO BE
      FOLLOWED!
      And projects an angered fingered hand
      Worn calloused beneath the polyester
white jumpsuit
      His toes curling in patent leather jackboots
While Null stands at the side,
Unable to contain himself
      And thinking, -My, doesn't that starship look
just like an old passenger plane missing its wings?
      And knowing the secret, all the while, that
the Captain is a Prince in a family line
Who were decimated by alien scourge in some epic

genocidal travesty,
Some great stab in the dark
And Null intones -I'll tell you a secret...
And the raw face of the Pyramid Head
almost shows surprise,
And the Captain looks at him in a single
light speed click of cosmic tension,
And I wonder...

Visions O' Great River (Hell on One Bank, Heaven on the Other)

Outside of a shopping mall
A camp of pre-fab buildings
And computer terminals sits
Fenced-in by want
Inmates dying of loneliness, confusion
A sense of displacement
Apparently I was permitted to leave
Maybe I went wandering around the mall
Which seems like it has become some post-
apocalyptic shelter
Or morphed into a school or prison
Or purgatory of some sort
Back outside, remembering the frustration.

            sitting at the terminals, trying to work
programs
 Obscure and arcane
            In data languages little minds can't process
(or maybe this is all just obsolete)
 Our bug-infested machines a fire hazard from
1983?
            After a return from indoors
            The world has grown dark as
            The hand of God
            While I fix my eyes on the camp in the
distance
Towering columns of thick black smoke
Wafting up to the inky sky
            As a large boy wanders around
            His black hair covering the gloom of his
Flabby visage
            I look down the hill at a new camp
 A fenced-in corral of bright color and light
 In heavy contrast to our drab, tormented place;
            -We've been struck by the Hand of God, he
says, looking up with a bitter grin.
            Down there, I can see the glow from the
computer terminal screens,
            Moved a if by -The Hand of God
Or maybe the smug little things have a mind of
their own.
            -We're damned, at any rate, I think Johnny

Cash once told a story about his dying brother
        Who was cut apart by a band-saw in a
workroom accident
        And lingered at the point of death for days
While the family prayed around him
 And he had visions
        Of a great river, with Heaven on one bank
And Hell on the other.

Some Fell Among Thorns

        We were driving past the college, and
Auntie lean out the window and say,
        -You see her over there?
        And I turn and spy her,
        some old woman
        sitting cross-legged in back of a building
must be
        one hundred years old.
        And my vision sweeps up
        and around her as we pass.
        -That's a strange sight for a residential
neighborhood.
        -Place has fallen on hard times. Except for
the college. It just keeps getting bigger and bigger.
        -I wonder, I say, if that's the girl they say
pretend to be dead. Like she trying to make a point

about something.

    -About time, maybe?

    She is squatting

    as if somebody plop a mushroom

underneath her.

    No emotion,

    just a stiff, cold stare like a crouching

shopwindow

    mannequin

    of a hundred years previous.

    She could be meditating

    on the nature of her own death, for all I

know.

    -But some girl dress like that and pretend to

go all stiff. Or that she is a ghost or something.

Or maybe time double back on itself. What you

think she is saying, Auntie?

    -Some fell among thorns?

    -You've been quoting that all day.

    Later,

    walking across an open court

    or parking lot on campus,

    I hear the most wretched, tuneless singing,

really screaming,

    coming from a kid with double rows of

spiked red hair and a white shirt

    open at the collar-nice clothes, really.

    Not punk clothes.

The kid is screeching angry
punk rock songs
he's listening
to over his headphones.
He walk alone in the distance, a ball of
tension.
Crossing my path
is a man in a three-piece business suit,
brown, with a briefcase and blonde hair; shoulder
length.
He has a tall, thin frame.
At first, I make he is a burn victim.
Someone has replaced
the skin of his face
with some sort of macabre latex covering.
It approximates human features, covering
something skinnier,
uglier, squirming beneath the surface.
Something thoroughly alien; something
that must be hidden
at all costs...

Auntie's Beach

The beach was a long,
snake-like strip of sand leading up to two
sandcastle thrones perched atop a little pyramid
of jagged rock.

The tide was coming in.

-But this is not the sea, Auntie, He say.

He is bent over in the surf.

She is bent over

as well.

Beside them, a dripping wet notebook of scrawled chicken-scratches

plays lazily in the gentle tide.

The pages are still barely readable, if he could make out her handwriting.

Sand is sticking on the

pages

She is bent over, hunched, in a miserable position.

Defeated,

like a depressed monkey.

-I once saw a monkey eat a piece of rotten fruit to get drunk, he say. He say this as if it is the most fascinating fact in all the world. I think he saw it on National Geographic.

She looks at him miserably.

-You probably just dreamed that, she says. She is still squatting in the sand and foam.

-No. But I'll tell you what I did dream last night.

She looks at him

with those miserable, bleary red eyes.

Her hair is a limp, wet, frazzled mess.

She says,

-And what did you dream last night, Null?

She says this as if she couldn't care less.

He spy the mysterious,

spiral bound notebook a few feet away, where it is gradually becoming more and more soggy and ruined by the salt sea.

The steady churning slop of the incoming tide lulls me into a semi-trance.

-Last night I impersonated Hitler.

She stares blankly, uncomprehending.

-Of course, I had on a stiff grey Nazi jacket with a swastika armband, and I had a cartoon approximation of Hitler's face and famous limp forelock. The dream began in the middle of events, I think.

-I was delivering a speech when, suddenly, an assassin stands up in the crowd, points a Walther P.38 at me, and fires...or maybe it was a row of assassins. I can't remember. At any rate, I can still see the determined, square-jawed visage of the lead assassin, his hair combed over into his eyes. I tell you: it could have been a young Hitler.

-But I was hit. But not killed. Next I know, I am recuperating in a schoolroom restroom, a big place. But the stall I'm stuck in doesn't seem to have a door. So here I am, sitting with my pants down around my ankles, and I'm sure I've shit myself from being shot, and I'm bleeding still, minimally.

-And this row of horrid teenage girls comes rushing in in a line, and right away I make they are trying not to look at my bloody, shitty nakedness, and they are retrieving book bags or packs from a big pile in a corner of the lavatory. I am still dressed as Hitler, and the whole situation just seemed monstrous.

-So I must have beat a retreat from a lavatory to a dormitory room. I am talking to two Jewish boys about Hell. I seem as if I don't believe in Hell. I ask, So where is this Hell you speak of?

-One of the boys seems shy and withdrawn. The other is a chubby fellow in a white T-shirt and a sock cap. He has a dark complexion and wide, laughing eyes.

-I ask him if only Jews go to heaven.

-He affirms this for me.

-So I stumble out, shot. I'm still dressed as Hitler apparently, still bleeding, although why I haven't bled to death yet I its own private mystery.

-So this monster truck that looks like a UPS truck crossed with a house on wheels comes pulling up.

My mother is behind the wheel. She looks a lot younger. Hitler's mother was young when she died.

And inside it is huge, and gunmetal grey
floors.

Looks like a giant storehouse.

-And I tell her all about being Hitler. Got me
shot. I'm bleeding all over these floors.

***

He looks up from his reverie.

Up the beach,

he can see his grandparents

seated imperiously on thrones made like
sandcastles.

They are either asleep,

petrified into suspended animation, or
dead.

But their expressions seem frozen in time.

He looks back at his aunt.

She is still crouched in the surf.

Beyond, he can see the sun darken behind
little

grey and white veil of cloud, revealing its
face only momentarily to paint with bright yellow
illumination the seashore world.

Below,

that damnable soggy notebook

clotted with sand, soaked through until the
scrawled loops of ink were blotted into nonsense,

(--It had something to do with a bundle of sticks.)

He didn't know what she was talking about; she looked as if she was recovering from some sort of mental fugue state. Or maybe just coming down off of really good drugs.

She ran her fingers through her stringy, dirty bangs. Overhead, lonely gulls cast shadows on the ground below.

***

Later

he walked up the beach,

Kicking driftwood as he went. His sneakers were clotted with sand; his nose was stinging with the rasp of sea salt. He had sweated a bit, but felt surprisingly cool as the gentle breeze wafted in off the water.

Ahead, he saw the strange, statuesque figures of his maybe dead grandparents seated in their sandcastle thrones.

-It's a lesson of some sort. Something about time?

He wasn't sure. Seagulls cawed; the tide rumbled less and less gently. Sandcastles eroded in the salty air.

It was all a moment.

Mama Blowin' in the Breeze

She sent her out,

(to play,
 one day
in May;)

And in the ceiling, by hook or by crook;
Next to the nook,
Where they cook...

======================================
==========

It was one dip of road,
 going down to the brown,
 crown / of the house
Like a mouse

(she scampered across fields and yards)
 where tricycle rusted in the Midwestern breeze
unfettered louse
 (And I can't believe)
And she wore the sunshine like dappled green
(a crown)

And the light sent tall shadows down,
(a diadem a rose for the hanging body)

in death's repose

in the noose suspended
Across the fields
(The shadow painted across kitchen floor)
as baby comes back inside the door
for lunch
(and cartoons promise that even nightmares
sometimes have an ending...)
And there's a human being
(holding fast)

Like "angels farting on the ceiling..."

And the little eyes
(look up in wonder)
Without tears
for now, for now, for now....

Part 2: Some Recent Poems

Where Have You Been, John Redhawk?

THE PLACE

For all the world, it looked almost like a South African squatter camp: a few rusted tin shacks blowing in the dust of the hot Autumn breeze.

Intermixed were a smattering of green, white, and even pink trailers baking beneath the moonlight. Some bore the evidence of th hustles offered within: painted mystics, bearded ladies, various sordid delights in the form of naive art. A bearded swami holding forth over a trio of tarot cards; large blazing letters that read "Fortunes," and "Horoscopes," and even "Palms Read Here."

"Someday," he said, looking up at the vast canopy of stars overhead. "I'll punch a hole in the sky. I'll fly on out, over the left shoulder of God. And then, I'll be free."

But that had been ten years ago, and nobody had seen him since.

"Where would you go, John Redhawk? Where?" she had asked. Her rawbone face stretched ugly and narrow and bleak with its own delighted look. Inside she was laughing at him.

"Here," she said, "Everybody dies. All the time. We all die. Just a little bit, more and more every day. I'm turning grey."

Actually, her splotchy, bug-stained and bug-bit legs were as white as cheese; Under the filmy, pale dress of soft, powder blue; pale because being washed and bleached and dried under the unforgiving rays of a godless sun.

"Some indian," she laughed. Hefted the bottle of hooch and passed it on to John, who was bald with red hair spilling out over the ears.

He hefted the bottle. He was leaving.

Her face was a bleary, laugh-and-tear-streaked mask ; hair spilling out in two feathered lumps of grease across the forehead; forehead also the color of cheese. Her breasts were tiny lumps beneath the blouse, wound around like a snake sunning itself in the moonlight, revealing the bra strap of one shoulder.

Hussy.

But he did it anyway. And then disappeared.

THE FUNERAL

They buried Mitzy in back, in a place where people dumped old tires and tin cans, porno books and slick fuck mags and trash to burn. Fires blazing in rusted garbage cans flaking poison fragments like dead skin, into the soil.

There were no officiating padres to deliver imprecations to an uncaring G-d.

"We should put him on trial," someone suggested.

"Who?"

"G-d."

The clowns cavorted and the the mystics mystified.

A shovel full of earth thrown over the shoulder.

As

They lowered her down.

"And you know this is illegal dumping, right?"

Said someone In The Know, about such things.

"Yeah. But won't nobody care in a hundred
years."

And a boy said, his shitty drawers drooping
around his chalk-white ass,

"Where's John Redhawk. Weren't he and her?"

"What?" asked Spangles the Clown.

"Lovers?"

And Spangles, nearly aglow asked, "Where
indeed?"

And Bobo, who remembered something John
once told him said, "He's flown off. He's going to
punch a hole in the sky."

"Someday," he forgot to add.

THE RETURN

The time is ticking swiftly by.

The night has blackened out the sky.

A lonely streetlight sees a man go by...

In the deep well of shadow he is painted head to
toe, with knapsack thrown over his shoulder, his
boots send up titan splashes of mud and earth as
his steps eat up the gravel track of the midway,
through the ugly little camp.

It's been raining, is still wet, and the drip-drip
from tin is a counterpoint to his breathing,

As he knows that only sleep can cure the ills of
his heart.

And he manages to make it to a cabin made of

corrugated tin hammered together in the black
heart of forgotten hopes and dreams.
Knock, knock...
Bobo comes to the door with a mouth full of
beans. Opens. Does a double-take at the long, lean
man in the dirty jacket,
With the dripping hair,
"Where have you been, John Redhawk?"
But the man stands there, on the threshold
Of a cheap trailer house, and he rears back his
head to laugh,
But he is really looking in the dripping darkness,
Past the clown,
Into the years,
Back through the shadowed years.
He says, finally,
"We did this before, didn't we? A hundred years
ago."
Bobo can't answer but asks,
"Did you?"
To which the man replies, "Sure. Finally. I
punched that hole in the sky."

Church Bells

It is a bright summer day when a little boy
Carries a mason jar of water
to the side of an Indiana house,
baking
Out in the summer sun so long ago. (Squatting

naked in the bright white glow of yesterday's noon times.)

"Granpa Atop a Rickety Ladder,"

(Like a Norman Rockwell scene of American Peach Pie Eisenhower-era goodness.) leaning at crazy angles it is.

Over the side of the house a comfortable swell of belly / and blue jeans paint-flecked--Bespattered, with precious white drops

while little man goggles to pass the liquid up. And the rose bushes curl across the patio / Like pythons in the bright,

The grandpa wears a billed cap and sunglasses, although LARGE, ROUGH DIRTY HANDS

Whisk white the old brush across the cracked and porous surface of the dawn.

"You'll talk my ear off," he say, but he can't remember a single, solitary sentence / That quivered forth from eager childhood lips (it is a play and a satire on communication).

And ten years from now when I am dead, I'll go to wander the beak 1982 neighborhoods so vast and empty / As the sunrise beckons to graying porch

And...hear the bells.

(...as little man stands in the shadow of the church steeple.)

Grandpa in breast pocket suit as dead fingers shake tiny boy palm with four hideous sausage stumps. Ringing bells reverberate,

The factory town neighborhood wherein we gave birth

To gritty families under the shadow of

71

Antennas and rickety want.

(Is that the wedding bells of the Risen Christ?)

Over the street I go / and deserted, no cars (the last time this happened was on 9-11)/ and yards overgrown with crabgrass and abandoned tricycle in derelict yard

rusts in the wind and dew.

Nerf balls beckon, sad plastic junk toys left like lonely orphans

Where are the little fists to manipulate / the tiny fingers to press down?

Into the earth?

The good black soil to penetrate the spaces and crevices between naked toes?

Plastic junk garbage toys sad bottle left dead and empty / as an autopsied heart in the gravel pathway.

(But, someone on Sunday is praying.)

Bells, bells, bells, church, bells, bells, bells...

"Can you hear them still? Say, Granpa and a rusted enormous whale of a car, with a radio antenna, and those little knobs in the dash board face?--

Parked in the gravel slut in the front yard, by the side of the idle street sloping down / and clouds move over the sun.

A hill runs, intersecting, as if the humpback of a vast, subterranean serpent, buried and petrified, rests curled beneath the roadway.

Down to the three Dante Divine Comedy Mouths of the triple underpass / Above which, locomotive roars overhead and cuts, through the rumbling air, when life fades down to slumber behind peeking windows in the black.

Squat like decaying dollhouses of want under the Midwestern sky.

And then you hang a left,

Coming across, little by little whistling past the boneyard, / the IOOF--

craggy hills and dips, and old tottering monuments, generations of dust and bone buried beneath the soil of a faded day gone

long ago choked in the dust, with the worms that rule the body, devour the brain.

(...appropriate.)

The Pilot

The old man with the white whiskers,

Flies his little single-engine prop plane,

Perilously close to the road below, strafing a cowering auto

Which cuts through fields of dark corn, as behind us, behind him at least

(as I am mere passenger on his midnight aerial cruise)

The screaming erupts into the night, and I comment,

--Someone is being killed back there.

--But is this presently occurring, or just an echo?

He looks into the black, star-strewn sky above and tells me,

--I know.

And later, when I try to shower all the filth of him away,

The wizened old goat face with the straggling hair and beard lock me

In the hotel bathroom,

And I know that like a shower scene in a certain movie,

The next night's screaming will come from me.

"Rock Around"

"One two, three o'clock, four o'clock!"
(Drum rumbles and rat-a-tats. Horns rise.)
—and we is watching a film,
all lying like lazy leeches on couches
at A's old house, although he is gone five years
and cold in his grave.
—And the TV rumble farts a croon from Nick Cave,
about thank you girl, thank you girl
(and he draw out that "thank you" until it is
"thaaaaahnk yahhh, gurrrl!" Thaaaaahnk yahhh,
gurrrl!"; and, anyway, he'll love you and thank you
'Til the End of the World.")
—And Auntie and Dot-Dot are there,
and Auntie have on some tan sheen makeup
and big eyelashes (what make her look like a
mulato of tragic fame),
and they fall all crooked over her

74

big,

sleepy,

stupid,

(Pummeling walk of bass notes swell bigly.)

sin-filled and indelicate eyes.

—And she is like a teenage debutante,
huge, crooked, paste-on eyelashes
and she go out,
down the porch, stepping off the stone step
and he explode, and point the finger in the face
(like pointing the bone in voodoo);
and accuse her,
and ask her again why she violated a child at
eleven,
and tell her how sick and disgusted he is.
—And come back in and two hulking gang
members are getting ready to throw down,
with huge coats covering their gun bellies
—and one gets up, and says something to the
other,
who is threatening-like, but he do a little
embarrassed dance
...and get a look on his face like he break wind.
And I go to sleep,
and wake up

—and a cop

with a dog

on a leash

outside is wishing me back to wakefulness
as the red and blue lights flicker flaming
fireworks across the wall.
"Mr. Baker? Mr. Baker?"
(Electric twang of iron guitar. Someone has been
shot.)
—and Auntie and Dot-Dot are gone.
—and it's like last house on the left sez is:
"just a movie, just a movie, just a movie..."
—and it is called "Rock Around the Clock," and
Bill Halley and The Comets are there in spirit,
and the screen flash to an image of Eisenhower-
era illustration
of Squaresville:

Dad

and Mom,

and Jilly,

and Susie,

and (don't forget) Little Billy

—and America and Apple Pie and,
like wholesome goodness.
—and the audience get up to leave and laugh,
and they have enjoyed this time while the music

from another era,
  another age
  (manipulate the mind)
  —to take it back to another time
  and command the audience that they
  SHALL BE MERRY AND CONTENT CONSUMERS
  (and cheerful);
  ...and life is like a soap bubble that is already
burst
  but we just don't know it.
  YET.

In the Doorway

I see you standing there
in the doorway, my small demonic self
[as a reflection of me],
  What I was thirty years ago.
  But, not so, I want to absorb you like Bradley the
Buyer
  in *Naked Lunch*, or whoever sneaks up on the
spectral grey vapor-like transmission of junk sick to
  Steal the soul—"and why can't some horrid
character get physical a natural way?"
  But this is blather. You're not real; not what I
want or desire,
  Just an abstraction.
  I bend over in my BDUs so you can examine my
asshole.

79 Words and Perfect Fear

Daffy Duck launched
a tunnel to the sky
--Babel, Babylon, "Intolerance..."
    (Legend of 1916)
He gets going through space and time,
straight into the Mouth of God--
He is then sent back
down through his dimensional tunnel,
where he gets caught
in the claustrophobic hold of it.
God sends down a Dyson Ball of solid mud
to strangulate Daffy,
whose face strobes for the viewer in a cryptic,
dough-boy series
of macabre flashes,
looking like a tortured clay animation puppet.
I struggled up a hill
trying to find
TWENTY
additional words with which to complete this
Poem
After being put through literal hell
On the way down....
27, 27, 27, 27, 27...

(It is of singular note that this poem is actually
eighty words long. Unless I miscounted. But you
need a hundred.)

The Cloth-Covered Form

Last night, I dreamed I was holding the withered bones of an estranged relative in my arms, she being wound in her shroud. My mother, sitting in a chair with rotted teeth, a bleeding, infected mouth, begged me, 'Do not hold her thus!'; but I lie with her regardless, hearing her murmur, though she were dead.

Getting up, after the act of love, I put a cloth across her face.

'Angels see thee to thy rest.'

I had drained the life from this one; for, years ago, she had drained the life from me. I had loved her unto death.

The Window

Cold cars speed by below me—
The window looks down on a scene,
As rain drizzles the streets and the old friends
Gather at a table somewhere in the distant past.
Below, we are cold and alone, lost babes in the
womb of the electric night—
America, do you have blessings for us drunken
rabble
Purchasing a few moments warmth in the cold
bosom of a comfort that can never come?
Ghosts pound the pavement of my sleep, as fog
creeps around the corner—
And where is my love? Gone perhaps, salted

away in the misty murk of some yesterday remembrance of dreamed things as I pine for the soft touch of skin and caress of hair to blot out tomorrow's distractions.

I am a cold eunuch.

I touch the ice of minutes like an insect battening on the sugar of a sweet sunrise cavalcade—

Coffee murk of memory distracts me as I embrace the wanton image of my daydream—

This is night, and all I know is night, and electric streetlamp gives villainous testimony to bygone romance of the spirit—I am fractured and neutered—old and spent.

And the city is freezing. It could eat a hundred million units of warmth as bug men drive by in brash vehicles giving spinning tires squealing oratorios against cracked and frozen pavement of this one, precise, center of geographical space which has come to represent

Heaven, Nirvana, Shangri-La...

How many of you could I have loved?

How many disappeared like shadows after the fall of sunlight in the dry bitch morning's evil wake?

How many cold faces destroyed? Little boy, little girl, young man and woman, where did you run to and where are you going so quickly, speeding into the tapestry of a yesteryear that doesn't hold any interest in you?

I miss you. Won't you sit with an old man and ponder sad recollections over black coffee and burning smokes, and let us look out that window up and down a street that seems to have pulled in

the bosom of its life like some camouflaged
monster come in from an ocean deep?
   I can't reclaim you,
      Each one disappeared into the twisting smoke
of the clicking, ticking, damnable clock, that eats us
all everyone.
      I can't claim your bosom for my own, will never
own your lithe body, or feel your breath hot
against my neck, or know what it is to suck in your
life force vampiric as the darkness settles over
naked city flashing with the trash and neon blink of
burger joints and old bars.
   This world America is cold and plastic and
      Love is a stranger bent on his knees ready to
take it in the mouth from the forces of Reason—I
am an alien in a strange land—I am a walking
cadaver of your institutions and medications—but
human? Who could say?
   How I long to meld with your flesh, hideous
nightshade beauty,
   spectral phantom of my heated mind,
   and conjoined like parasitic twins
   dance the sweet nothings of a playful pile of
dust,
   blown like chaff in the limitless gale of an
October wind.
      What more could I want?
      I want you Past,
  to come back and reclaim me and give me the
minutes I am still living.
      You cheat.
      I know you.
      I still feel the minutes in my mind,

yet, they are gone as surely as if they had
disappeared up the hairy sleeve
   of a coldly calculating magician.
   I don't like this trick.
   Give me back beauty,
   Passion
   And the Night,
   And I will sweep the dirt from my bones
   and rise up to walk,
   like grey ghost through the backward streets
   in search of that one ineffable, unspeakable,
immutable experience of pure bliss.
   And that might be seen in a human face.
   And it might be felt in the twiggy grasp
   of soft fingers
   Peeling back my lizard skin
   for a sign of human warmth.

Beef

   Now, this story has little to do
   with cutting beef.
   But, I,
   in point of fact,
   was doing so.
   Standing upon a wheel,
   a wooden wheel,
   with a mountainous amount of raw beef
   laid out before me, and a sword in one hand.
   And, because I was starving,

in the other, slivers
of raw beef
I greedily stuffed
into my mouth.
"I can't... seem to get enough,"
say I, chewing
a huge cud of cow flesh.
And maybe the old woman is there,
(on bended knees.)
But I can only see her back, and she is scrubbing
the floor in this dirty, dirty kitchen, or whatever.
(The beef is growing huge, looping intestines
made of liverwurst. Braunschweiger.)
As eating raw beef
is not an omen that portends
well, we'll leave it right there.
(Outside, somewhere, in that fantastic way in
dreams wherein an individal can "bi-locate", I am
standing with a friend whom I'll call "Mac," a tall
rawboned man dressed like something that
crawled from a cockpit during WW2.)
The sun beams down on his face,
and his adulation seems reserved
chiefly for me.
Zipping above,
like a too-loud bumblebee
held aloft
by ribbon
and canvas
and glue,
the Old Man
is set to come zipping
down

into the field,
as tall grass waves like delicate
fingers in the gentle,
almost still wind.
"It's like a dune buggy with wings," says Mac. He
hefts a pair of binoculars to his rawboned face.
(And the late afternoon sun dips down to orange.
And all slips into infinite space and time.)

Last Call of the Wild Bird

I can still see you,
in the prison of my mind's eye,
Bedraggled
in your great black coat; eyes wide, staring at a
space beyond the darkness.
Wise and yet doomed
(—the last owl in the barn.)
At midnight, the clocks tick away, counting down
the moments until you take flight
(in that world of spirits
wherein yesterday still travels the dead pathways
of memory
with earthly feet.)
And somewhere,
screeching the shadowed eaves at sunset,
the
"Last Call of the Wild Bird,"
high piercing scream, perhaps;

but it could be a final round bought,
for old friends,
as you take flight again out of my memories,
and I drink a toast to happier times.

Kill Heyzeus

I was walking down a coffin-shaped hall,
thinking about the woman
Beyond the door
On the right.
...Ahead, the walls,
Ceiling,
And hallway all
converged
...to a single square backwall,
Chest-high; it was as if everything were being
sucked
into a window-shaped space
into some dimension beyond.
...But, of course, that was ridiculous.
The architecture might be arcane,
even occult.
But the back wall was still only that.

...in the next room,
The white walls
gleamed with a wash of bright sunshine
That seemed to be seeping in

From parts unknown.
That can't be the flourescents, I think.
The wooden floors were piled high
with detritus and refuse,
old papers and books and whatnot.
The old woman was sitting there,
her legs splayed out beneath her,
twisted

in an uncomfortable, unnatural fashion.
I assumed she was crippled
or, at least, injured.

I realized for the first time that this is a basement
area.
"How do we get upstairs?"
I asked the old woman.
Her head twisted around,
a macabre grin spreading across her face.
Short librarian hair, painted cheeks, ruby lips;
wild eyes.
"Kill Jesus!" she spat.
She was clearly insane, possibly possessed by
devils.
Or,
... maybe she was just talking about the
landscaper.

The Body of Ginsberg

I, or rather WE get off the train,
And it is a station of white walls,
white floor,
and sunshine
Slanting in but painting orange all around
as if by cheap florescent
God is illuminating this space for us.
And going by room after room,
in silence,
But for Vedic hymns chanted
via telepathy in soundproof cubicles...
She wants to go to lunch, but I say--
Come here. I have to show you--
And herein lies the Body of Ginsberg
which might be, as it were,
Wrapped in a cheap shroud,
a carnival-type mummy wrap
from some Chinese Isle that claims
Brahma
or Buddha
or Jesus of Nazareth
slept within its paltry threads
and adorned with the all-Pervading
One-Eyed Palm of Vishnu.
In a bed I say,
There he is I say,
What's become of him, she says...
And we move on.
Away from the window.
In that window, in the hospital bed,
Lies the Body of Ginsberg.
But not dead to the yogi chants
trying to win for him Moksha...

But alive,
as a stunted, rotted thing,
his impotent, leprous hands reaching up to
heaven,
in a muted prayer.
(Has someone strung their prayer beads across
the wall?)

Black Bird

What symbolism is at the bottom
Of a black bird (raven),
Squatting on a half-eaten buffet
(The table)
long after the dinner has commenced?
Or what of a dog running up the way,
Toward the glass door, and on his lips
a sneer as if to say,
—Master loved me before he knew I knew how
to talk.
And behind him , a wolf-hound snarls chasing,
leaping
with a skull-face plate mask over his
expressionless, hungry jaws.
(and this same dog was with us at the house),
At the House: Where a trio of corpses sang
"Halleluia," as this is the face-plate icon come
home hell-hound avenger of the Risen Christ.
And Black Dog is Satan, Lucifer, Belial,
Leviathan—
As befitting all the ancient tales of woe.

***

(And I think to myself, walking past, humming a ballad about King Arthur—My these pies and cakes left sitting out are going to make everyone ill.)

The Ballad of Meat Woman

Meet Woman, Meat Woman,
why did you die?
Rotting on the ground made of tuna and rye!
salami goes hungry
underneath the sky;
you're a mountain of cold-cuts and fat.
Meet Woman, Meat Woman,
hidden underground--
flesh-golems hear the funeral sound!
Chanting out pater-noster,
pound for pound--
on the cracked walk you still lie flat!

The snake and the bike,

in the cage,

with the priest,

survived a riot at the funeral feast!

And the communards

all ply their trade as

Jack the Ripper drips the love he made.

Meat Woman, Meat Woman
flesh debased--
I'll wrap you in cellophane and let you taste--
The honey-drip nectar
of my subtle ways,
lunchmeat-mama
drives the carnivore craze.

The fish in the hole

is hollow and bare--

and the cook with the oil in his jet-black hair--

fingers the cavity

of the thing,

as the day rolls on, and the jailbirds swing.

Meat Woman, Meat Woman
it's quite clear:
your shelf-life is over and the end is near.
As the buildings burn,
and the cops give chase--
I drop a drab of mayonnaise on your cold-cut

face!

Babel

A vast, limitless throng of prisoners walk the
slick, cement pathway upward; This could be the
Tower of Babel (scene from Metropolis, 1927).
Above me, a warder, (or turnkey)
wonders/wanders with his co-worker: "Why he
hates me to the degree that he does."
He has oily,
slicked-back hair, sideburns,
and a huge flat,
Ski-slope nossum;
really a bridge
going down, punctuating the
Upper lip assemblage.

He is dressed

in a white shirt:
plain street slacks,
unfettered by uniform wear.

And, as he cracks an invisible whip-hand flourish,
I make with my gun fingers (neither of us being
really, truly armed);
Point with my hands folded and the index finger
sticks out—BLAM! He goes down like a Tijuana
crack whore—And I note an interesting fact:

He is not a real man, but some sort of Hollywood prop—MANNEQUIN. (Perhaps inflatable?)

As he slides down the cement walkway, prisoners part to make room; and I realize THIS—

"That is the sort of thing they use to throw out of windows in bad movies."

At Carnival

Gentle leaves blow across Autumn yards pale as bone grass crunched under boot, and acrid smoke belches from old barrels full of newspaper and dry twigs.

Cold dust freezes in the lines of your face, making the leaning shadows of sunset seem like chilly fingers painting the dismay of all our hours bright.

Weeds fertile and tall straggle across open fields, where struggle of new blossoms die in the dark pall cast by the coming snow.

Children drink the nectar of air, rife with the cotton candy flavor of nightshade, and carnival hums like a brilliant hive of rainbow bees come in from a dream.

Brightly the tilt-a-whirl spins! Brightly the carnival banners blow! Bright the painted faces of Halloween leer, as darkness and the death of time descends.

Georgia

Red sunset swirls color of old orange flames
as the car dives between the line.
Hostages to fortune cower in the backseat.
When will nightfall?
Draining the dusty throat
on broken glass bottle that the mop man picks
up,
After stone cold negro trance mutters
with broken lip savoir faire "Hey muthafucka,
hey."
Cleaning the muck of the floor
and sliding
—down your throat,
(the peppers)
and heat curls like an untamed cobra into your
armpits,
And the darkness in here is broken
by jukebox tittering and rumble of
old pinball games
as we slide tables together
for a pool of food.

But outside.

OUTSIDE!!!

The psychopath leers into the peach sunset.
—Peach, peach, everything is peach.
The sky is peach, the earth is peach, the dusty old
eighteen wheel monster silhouetted against the

rays of flame
   is peach.
   Where are we going, sliding over the pitted,
   cratered surface of this non-terrestrial world,
   and you tell me about hotels in outer space?
   This mission is over.
   All color has been drained to pink.
   The heat is all we have left and the sunset.

To Johnny Who Thought He Would Never Die

   I remember sitting over coffee,
   Seeing your beautiful face
   Resplendent in the lowering gloom of afternoon
sunset.
   Lit by the damp electric--
   And you snicker that breathless little laugh
through your nose, and Johnny say to me he tell
me,
      "I'm never going to die."
   And arrogant I think and I say,
   But Johnny I have a poem in mind called:
      "To Johnny Who Thought He Would Never
Die."
   And you get a look on Johnny's red bearded face
like tears bubble and boil up. And fifteen years
later you disappear from your seat--empty--blank--
vamoose--gone--out of there, ya dig?
   And so I sit here fifteen years on, looking for

YOU, Johnny; and now you're raised up to the level of Holy Ghost; adventurer; Virgil; psychopomp; the Immortal Johnny, who walks resplendent with a halo of rumpled cap and a heavenly gown of dark trench coat.

(Like it was Two Thousand and Three.)

And when the lights blink out and this thing in my chest kills me finally, I'll walk the Jesus to Hell Expressway in a tunnel of Hollywood lighting, and reunion with relatives gone on before me; and I'll see YOU there, Johnny; shuffling, shambling, mumbling Johnny.

"There is Johnny."

"There was Johnny."

"There he goes."

(Psychopomp, writer, street magician...)

Behind me move souls twisting in the gentle breeze--

And I'll say,

"There's Gramma and Granpa, and Gramma and Grampa, and Auntie, and Cousin J."

And maybe I'll say to a woman in a wheelchair: "There's Mama."

But I should really stop all that.

Because, well, this poem is for JOHNNY.

Who Thought.

He Would Never.

Die.

Needles

I was with a large man,
a vegetarian activist--
scribbling madly in a notebook,
he referred to human infants as
"Useless eaters."
"What else would you call them?" he inquired.
And then two blonde women with butch cuts come
wading up the stream,
which is a deep gouge-like surgical scar through
the green,
overgrown brush.
And they have sacks full of grain
and I explain: That--
"Dogs
(And suddenly, a huge black mastiff is there
growing out of the weeds),
"DO NOT eat such things. But prefer a more
delectable, savory type of feed."
And they're just traveling on foot through
the murk of the tarn to
"Feed the animals."
And I tell them they should watch out
for used needles, dropped by junkies--
and other medical refuse.

The Mankey

There were a vast field of stray monstrosities,
stretching out from a line of billowing penants, to

the door of a small tent from where emerged a man with a monkey on a leash.

The man was dressed as a magician, with a top coat, stove pipe hat, and a curling moustache. His monkey was a large Macaw, chattering continually, pacing back and forth on its knuckles, agressively. Often he fed it a snack or a sweet meat, which it greedily and eagerly accepted. One who peered long in its simian face caught, in the gleaming, steady, dark gaze, a frightful and malign intelligence.

A number of families browsed through the field of curious straw idols, the extraterrestrial sentinels. One, an impressve fellow with one central trunk, a cephalapoid head opening into the painted impression of a huge, sinister red eye, was all the delight and desire of a young boy--who, quite unfortunately for him, was told that that particular idol was not for purchase, as it was the "Watchman" of the rest. The eye itself, incidentally, closed and opened with a straw lid or covering, pulled by a string.

The boy, whose famiy had wanted it for a conversation piece, was disappointed, but mollified him with a candy apple, and an ice cream, as to forestall the freckled cherub's tears. The red-headed angel would soon forget his oversized, desired toy, of course.

The curator of this weird display, or salesman, the Man With the Monkey, was rumored by some to be a scientist; a witch by others, doctor of fortune telling, perhaps, by others still; philosopher, perhaps. Some said he was an animal

98

trainer. Some wondered if the monkey, perhaps, were not his secret lover.

Both man and monkey shared sinister eyes. To meet their gaze was to be chilled, straight down to the marrow of your bones.

Raven Number 2

What is the symbolism of a raven,
Squatting
On a buffet table,
Long after the meal has commenced?

What a dog talking,
His telepathic breath
Blowing in the breeze?
As if to say,
--Once you loved me, Master,
But now you have your doubts?

Behind him the wolf hounds his heels,
Wearing a skull-face plate mask to impersonate,
The Risen Christ.

Also Available

Kluge:

Based on a True Story

Tom Baker

Kluge by Tom Baker

Kluge lives with his mother and brother in a tenement, in a nameless city, long ago. A misfit, a loner, Kluge lives in a fantasy world, until the day the dream ends, and reality reveals itself to be a nightmare. Discovering a terrible secret, Kluge explodes in a torrent of homicidal rage. Kluge lashes out at a world that mocks him, erupting in blood-spattered fury. But, is it all just another of his dreams? This hardboiled novelette was written in a white heat of inspiration, based on a grisly true crime case from the Roaring Twenties. Kluge bristles like tough poetry. You'll never forget it.

54 Pages. ISBN # 9780359103003 6.00 USD

Made in the USA
Coppell, TX
01 July 2020